THE BRETHREN

a historical and theological review

200th Anniversary Edition

1825-2025

The past places us on a path,

to determine its destination,

we must understand it well.

CONTENTS

INTRODUCTION

Those who call themselves Brethren trace their roots to a movement in the early 1800s. At that time there was no label, no definition, nor any signs that would suggest that the early days would bear the fruit that we now see. Like a small stream that has no concept of it ending as a river, so those who bore within them the seeds of the movement were not aware of the impact they would bring. Movements never just happen; they are conceived because the circumstances are right, and they take shape within an environment that provides the right space and conditions for their growth. It was from the seedbed of apostasy and sectarianism, revival, and a deep desire for unity, that the Brethren movement began. A movement which although at first a mere stream would become a significant river.

As a member of this movement, I stand far downstream. From such a point the source and original energy of the movement becomes easily forgotten and distorted, to the point that questions like: "Where did we come from? What does it mean to belong to this movement? What was the intended direction of the movement?" and "Where does this river go to from here?" rise loudly.

In an endeavour to uncover answers to some of these questions one must first go back to the source of the movement, to the early 1800s, and there begin to understand the context in which the movement was conceived. Then seek to capture as far as is possible the heartbeat of the founders that forged the story of the Brethren movement. Because this work is primarily concerned with the passion that brought about the genesis of the movement, we will confine ourselves to only the early years of the Brethren. Having found the original passion and foundation, we will consider the founders' theology and practice from the vantage point of being removed from the original context and being far removed from the pervading theology of the day. In doing so we seek to find that which belongs to the context of the day, and that which is timeless and onto which the Brethren of today should hold and pass on to future generations.

HISTORY

THE SCENE

From 1533 and the separation of the Church of England from Rome, by Henry VIII, there had been only one recognised church in England, the Church of England. It was a state church, receiving its position, strength and power, from its establishment by the State. One may initially think that the Brethren movement was essentially borne out of a reaction to the apostasy of the Church of England at that time. While this is true it is only part of the story.

Prior to the Brethren movement, England had been host to at least three former renewal movements. The first, the Puritans, aimed to purge the Church of England of anything Roman Catholic. The Puritans of the 1560s contended that "too many rags of popery were still in the Anglican Church. ... Their main objections were directed against the continued use in the liturgy of the church of ritual vestments that seemed popish to them. They opposed the use of saints' days, clerical absolution, the sign of the cross, the custom of having godparents in baptism, kneeling for communion, and the use of the surplice by the minister" (Cairns, 1996, p. 328). In the 1570s under Thomas Cartwright the Puritan movement shifted its focus from the reform of liturgical elements within the church to the reform of its theology, insisting on the final authority of Scripture. While achieving much they failed to establish an accepted Puritan Church. Many Puritans left England for America in search of religious freedom. Many of those who remained formed dissenting congregations, later becoming known as Congregationalists (of these a large number migrated to Plymouth) and Independent Baptists.

The Quaker movement took shape under George Fox for whom Christianity was a "mystical experience in which one could come directly to God" (Cairns, 1996, p. 381). Under Fox's leadership, the Society of Friends (also called Quakers), was formed in 1652. Robert Barclay the theologian for the movement believed that "the Spirit was the sole Revelator of God and the source of 'Inner Light' within man that gave him spiritual illumination. The Bible was but a secondary rule of faith, and the inspiration of the writers was placed on the same level as the inspiration of Fox or any other Quaker" (Cairns, 1996, p. 381). Quakers were given to zealous evangelistic endeavours and their persecution by the authorities forced the spread of their work throughout England and abroad. They were noted for their strong missionary focus and their dedication to social service.

The third renewal movement prior to the genesis of the Brethren was that which became known as the Methodist revival. This revival initially took place within the Church of England. John Wesley together with his brother Charles met with other Anglican students at Oxford to further their devotion to God through a disciplined method of spiritual improvement, which included regular times of prayer and Bible study. This "Holy Club" at Oxford, grew following John Wesley's conversion in 1738, which was influenced greatly by the reading of Luther. He began to preach in Bristol, and from there on horseback around the country, creating what became known as the Methodist revival. Aspects which contributed to this revival were the development of a more enthusiastic preaching event, the use of hymns, the development of Bible study groups, and extempore teaching. Wesley resisted breaking from the Church of England. It wasn't until 1795, after Wesley's death, that the Methodist Church was formed outside the Church of England. There remained within the Methodist Church an Anglican influence on Episcopal polity, the reception of communion, and the separation of clergy and laity. However, they stressed "justification by faith through an instantaneous experience of regeneration . . . and the possibility of absolute Christian perfection in motive in this life because the love of God so filled the heart of the believer that God's love would expel sin and promote absolute holiness of life" (Cairns, 1996, p. 386).

We turn now to the more obvious contributor to the environment leading to the Brethren movement, the state of the Church of England. At the turn of the 19th century the Church of England was the only official church in England. All other religious formations were considered dissenters and sects and viewed by the official church as irreligious. Those who had been affected by renewal in any way had no real choice. They could leave the official church and be viewed in this way or remain within the church, which to many was in a deplorable state. "One contemporary critic described the Church of England as a 'machine of Anti-Christ' and looked forward to... when the establishment would be abolished by an Act of Parliament and put on an equality with the other Christian sects tolerated in this country. The Anglican bishops were accused of corruption and of neglecting their religious duties in the favour of lucrative business pursuits. The laity was almost completely excluded from any involvement in the spiritual matters of the church. The sermons given within the church drew the criticism of lacking life, predominantly because a display of enthusiasm within a sermon was viewed as being Methodist and regarded as an ecclesiastical misdemeanour" (Rowdon, 1967, p. 4). William Soltau, who later joined the Brethren, said of the preaching of the state church in that period that "he could not remember hearing a clear presentation of the evangelical message" (Rowdon, 1967, p. 5).

While the state of the Church of England promoted a mind of dissent, the growing popularity of the renewal movements provided a more flexible and attractive alternative. "Dissenting churches were on the whole, more flexible, and were beginning to throb with the new spiritual life generated by the Evangelical Revival of the late eighteenth century" (Rowdon, 1967, p. 3). However, the dissenting churches themselves also gave cause for concern among many. Within the dissenting churches there were growing tendencies toward clericalism and social sophistication, together with an ever-increasing sectarian approach to the Church of England which eventually began to create internal sectarian problems, resulting in the proliferation of dissenting groups. There soon became the situation in which "the established church had unity (at least from their own perspective) but did not have purity. On the other hand, the dissenting churches had purity (from their viewpoint), but they did not have unity. They claimed to be the true church because they were pure, yet the by-products of their stance were division and a sectarian attitude. The established church, for its part, claimed to be the true church because of its unity, accusing all the others of creating schisms. The by-products of its unity were cold theology and corruption" (Smith, 1986, p. 25).

The Brethren movement was not a unique and original movement but a product of the ingredients of the past movements and reactions to the surrounding churches of the day. It will become clear from the genesis story of the Brethren which follows, that the movement carried with it shades of Puritanism in its insistence on the authority of the Bible, of the Quaker movement with its zeal for missions and social service, and of Methodism with its emphasis on extempore preaching and its desire for purity. Also, many aspects of the movement were shaped through their reaction against the Anglican clergy/laity division, its lifeless form and structure, its apostasy, and its lack of evangelism. The Brethren also reacted to the clericalism and social separation, which the dissenting churches were creating. It was within this environment of renewal culture, sectarianism, and apostasy, that the Brethren movement took root and grew in the hearts of those who believed that God and Scripture called them to something other.

THE STORY

The story of the genesis of the Brethren begins in around 1825 when a number of groups began to meet on weekdays, "breaking bread together to express their unity" (Grass, 2012, p. 22). From there the story grows through a number of prominent men whose thoughts and actions solidified in the formation of three major centres of Brethren activity over a number of years. It is in the early 1820s to the late 1840s, that we seek through the thought and work of these men and the churches they led, to uncover the heartbeat, which gave life to the Brethren movement. It is in the heartbeat of these people and churches, in the early days, that one will find the truest passion of the movement, prior to any focus on the development of a tradition, which occurred later. It is here in this period of history that the formational principles and identity of the Brethren are to be found.

GROVES

Anthony Noris Groves (1795-1853) was a man with a big and compassionate heart, a man for the people. As a dentist he first practiced in Plymouth and moved to Exeter. In Exeter, through the influence of two clergy friends, he set his heart upon missionary work, offering himself to the Church Missionary Society. Upon marrying, however, he found his wife opposed to any missionary work. Consequently, all plans for such service were abandoned, and his heart became heavy. With the loss of his vision, Groves was heard to say "Often did I, with every earthly thing that man could desire, feel most miserable. I had a wife who loved me, dear little children, and a most lucrative profession, yet I had not the Lord's presence as in days past, and therefore I was miserable" (Coad, 1968, p. 16).

During this time Groves became self-conscious about his wealth, and being a compassionate man was convicted regarding his generosity. Groves and his wife determined to give a tenth of their income to the needy within their locality. This decision and the resulting involvement of Groves' wife in the distribution to the needy began to change her heart toward mission work. In light of the need she saw, it was decided that they should give away a quarter of their income. "It was not long before this decision also was revised, and the Groveses began to give all their income, beyond modest immediate needs, to the service of God" (Coad, 1968, p. 17). Groves' convictions in this regard grew beyond being personal, publishing his views in 1825 stating that "the deliberate accumulation of wealth is a plain hindrance to personal piety: indeed, he considered that there existed a clear duty to spend all one's goods in the service of God. . . . The Christian motto should be – labour hard, consume little, give much, and all to Christ" (Coad, 1968, p. 17).

The magnanimity of the Groveses was further expressed by Mary Groves, who began to support her husband's desire for missionary work. In July 1825 Groves contacted the Church Missionary Society and was accepted as a candidate for Baghdad. To prepare for his missionary future, Groves commenced a theological degree at Trinity College, Dublin. Apart from his training, this move introduced two important events into his life. Firstly, Groves' studies took him frequently to Dublin, the birthplace of the Brethren movement, where he met many who became the founders of the movement. Secondly, he employed Henry Craik as a tutor to help with his theological studies. Craik later became a prominent figure in the beginnings of the Brethren.

Groves, an Anglican, had for many years enjoyed the friendship and the study of the Scriptures with two non-conformist ladies, the Misses Paget. This association and their influence "was affecting him deeply as to the tragedy of Christian divisions" (Coad, 1968, p. 19). While in Dublin he came across a minority Protestant group that met for Bible study and discussion without any denominational barriers. Here Groves became aware of the disparity between the unity, freedom and fellowship of the apostolic church in comparison with the current condition of the church. In this circle of Christians who met in Dublin, Groves came in contact with a lawyer called John Bellett and a young curate named John Nelson Darby.

Under the influence of these meetings Groves views were maturing. In 1827 Groves stated to Bellett that "it appeared to him from Scripture, that believers, meeting together as disciples of Christ, were free to break bread together, as their Lord had admonished them; and that, in as far as the practice of the apostles could be a guide, every Lord's day should be set apart for thus remembering the Lord's death, and obeying his parting command. ... This suggestion of Mr. Groves was immediately carried out" (Coad, 1968, p. 20). According to Bellett, Groves was "the first to propose that simple principle of union, the love of Jesus, instead of oneness of judgement in minor things, things that may consist with a true love to Jesus" (Coad, 1968, p. 20).

Even so, Groves remained a strict Anglican churchman until the end of 1827. Groves was a pacifist, believing that this was what Scripture taught. He was faced at the end of his training, intending to go into missionary work, with the prospect of having to sign article 37 of the church, which commands Christian men to take up arms. Groves could not in good conscience sign it and thus his connection with the Church of England ceased.

Groves still intended to go to the mission field, not as a clergy man but as a layman, having refused ordination from the church. However, the Church Missionary Society informed him that he would be unable as a layman to celebrate communion with any in the mission field. This posed a problem for Groves until he came to the understanding that ordination was not a requirement of Scripture. So Groves and his wife left the church and left for Baghdad without affiliation with the Church Missionary Society. Groves' motto was to "accept all who Christ had accepted" and not to place any system of men in the way of Christian unity in the Lord. Groves was to write in his diary in 1834 of his experiences and thoughts: "I am so sure of the truth of those blessed principles the Lord has taught me that I glory in their propagation. Simple obedience to Christ alone; recognition of Christ alone in my brother, as the Alpha and Omega of terms of communion; lastly, unreserved devotion to Christ alone" (Coad, 1968, p. 24).

Groves sought a renewal of the church but without the condemnation of the existing system. He said, "I acknowledge the system to be wrong, very wrong, yet my heart finds great repose in those fair pearls which lie within, what seems to me, so naughty a shell" (Rowdon, 1967, p. 291). Groves sought union at all levels without condemnation at any level. He stated most clearly his views on church in a letter entitled 'On the Principles of Union and Communion in the Church of Christ', "in three propositions:

1.   We should love all individuals whom Christ loves.

2.   We should normally worship with the most Scriptural congregation.

3.   We may worship with any congregation under heaven where he manifests Himself to bless and to save" (Rowdon, 1967, p. 291-292).

While never an active leader of a "Brethren Assembly" Groves was in a real sense the father of the movement, the one who planted the seeds. To the Brethren movement Groves contributed a renewed commitment to mission work, self-generosity, and sacrifice for the poor and socially underprivileged. He called all to focus on unity in the Lord, and to find a freedom of fellowship at his table without the imposition of man-made systems of ordination and the like, thus destroying the clergy/laity division.

DARBY & DUBLIN

Groves stayed in the house of John Bellett (1795-1864) when journeying to Dublin to complete his quarterly exams at Trinity. Groves' time with Bellett left an incredible mark on him. Bellett was taken with Groves' idea on unity and freedom to break bread in the name of the Lord alone. Bellett was part of the group, which acted upon Groves' suggestion of such a communion service in 1827, in Dublin. Bellett was also impacted by another statement by Groves in 1828 (just prior to Groves' departure to the mission field). Regarding this statement by Groves to Bellett, Professor Basil Willey stated: "At this very time Congleton and Groves received a joint communication, of a mystical character, concerning the mind of God towards them: 'that we should come together in all simplicity as disciples, not waiting on any pulpit or minister, but trusting that the Lord would edify us together, by ministering as he pleased and saw good from the midst of ourselves' " (according to Rowdon, 1967, p. 40). "This revelation ... was the basis of Plymouth Brethrenism!" (Coad, 1968, p. 29). These two statements to Bellett by Groves according to Rowdon "sum up the basic insights into the nature of the church life which were to characterise the movement..." (Rowdon, 1967, p. 41).

James Nelson Darby (1800-1882) graduated from Trinity College in Dublin in 1819 as a Classical Gold Medallist. Darby began work as a lawyer on the Irish Bar but soon left his legal career for a life in the Church. He was ordained as a priest in 1826, becoming the curate of Calvary in County Wicklow. Soon after his appointment to that position in 1827, the Church of England required all clergy within the church to uphold the concept of English domination. This was received with obvious hostility from the Irish clergy. It however served as a catalyst for change in Darby's thinking on the church. In the same year he had a horse accident which provided him with a time of reflection on many issues during his recovery. Darby concluded "that the church of God, as he considers it, was composed only of those who were so united to Christ.... The careful reading of Acts afforded me a practical picture of the early church, which made me feel deeply the contrast with its actual present state" (Coad, 1968, p. 28). It was at this time that Darby came into contact with Bellett, both of whom had not yet broken with the Church of England.

Darby's thinking was consolidated, perhaps from his encounter with Bellett who had been greatly influenced by Groves, perhaps through his time of convalescence, and surely through his dissatisfaction with the state of the church and the proliferation of the dissenting groups. He recorded his thoughts in 1828 in what has become known as the first Brethren pamphlet, "The Nature and Unity of the Church of Christ." Its main focus was the despair over the disunity and apostasy of the church, and the search for a new basis for the church. In seeking the mind of Christ, Darby states:

"It was the purpose of God in Christ to gather in one all things in heaven and on earth; reconciled unto himself in Him; and that the church should be, though necessarily imperfect in his absence, yet by the energy of the Spirit the witness of this on earth. ... Believers know that all who are born of the Spirit have substantial unity of mind, so as to know each other, and love each other, as brethren. ... And true unity is the unity of the Spirit, and it must be wrought by the operation of the Spirit. He felt that no meeting, which is not framed to embrace all the children of God in the full basis of the kingdom of the Son, cannot find the fullness of blessing, because it does not contemplate it – because its faith does not embrace it. ... In the name of Christ, therefore they enter ... and in him alone can we find this unity. ... 'I, if I be lifted up from the earth, will draw all men unto me' ... It is then Christ who will draw – will draw to Himself (and nothing short of or less than this can produce unity. ... In a word, we find his death is the centre of communion till his coming again and in this rests the whole power of truth. Accordingly, the outward symbol and instrument of unity is the partaking of the Lord's supper – for we being many are one bread, one body for we are all partakers of that one bread. ... Accordingly, the essence and substance of unity ... is conformity to his death...."

"Further unity is the glory of the church; but unity to secure and promote our own interests is not the unity of the church... Unity that is of the church, is the unity of the Spirit, and can only be perfected in spiritual persons. ... Professed churches (especially those established) have sinned greatly in insisting on things indifferent and hindering the union of believers, and this charge rests heavily on the hierarchies of the several churches. ... But what are the people of the Lord to do? Let them wait upon the Lord, and wait according to the teaching of his Spirit, and in conformity to the image, by the life of the Spirit, of his son. ... The unity of the church cannot possibly be found till the common object of those who are members of it is the glory of the Lord..." (Darby Vol. 1, 1971, p. 23-34).

According to Miller we may consider the pamphlet to be a statement of what the growing community in Dublin believed and came to practice and present, becoming "the divine ground upon which they acted. It may also be considered to contain nearly all the elements of those distinctive truths, which have been held by Brethren from that day..." (Miller, n.d., p. 13-14). It is obvious that Darby felt the agony of a church divided and in many quarters its subservience to secular authorities.

From 1825 onward, there were a number of groups of Christians meeting together in Dublin, comprised of those who could not in good conscience find a suitable place to worship. In 1829 Darby and Bellett met in the home of Hutchinson who was "quite prepared to have communion in the name of the Lord with all, whomsoever they might be, who loved him in sincerity" (Coad, 1968, p. 29). A number from the various groups met to discuss the situation. Having arranged a time when all could meet outside other church commitments, Bellett, Brooke, Cronin, Darby, and Hutchinson, planned to gather to celebrate communion in Hutchinson's home, in Fitzwilliam Square. Many from the other groups meeting at the time began to join with the group in Hutchinson's home. In May 1830 the group decided that they should no longer hold the group as a private gathering but search for a more public place, where also those of poorer standing would not be embarrassed to meet (Hutchinson's home was that of a wealthy man). They hired a hall in Augier Street, Dublin, seen as the first meeting place of the Brethren, which through Darby began to formulate more concretely the beliefs which would mark the Brethren movement.

There was a problem, however. How could this group by setting up a new gathering avoid the label of dissenters, the very thing

Darby sought to fight? Darby concluded that the unity he sought should be centred around Christ alone, symbolised in the partaking of the Lord's Supper and in conforming to the death of Christ. This he saw as the objective and call of the church and every Christian. He further held that "Christians have a direct title to meet together to break bread – and if this is dubbed schism, then it ceases to be schism when it is schism from that which is worldly" (Coad, 1968, p. 34). Darby felt that in meeting around the Lord's Supper as commanded he was not breaking from the church, but from the world, which the church had joined and had thereby become apostate.

Later on, Darby through his interest in prophecy, firmed in his idea that the church as he saw it had in fact become worldly and that he must therefore break from the world and from anything worldly. Darby's "growing conviction that the kingdom of God would be established on earth as a result, not of the exertions of men on its behalf, a widely held view at the time, but of the direct intervention of Christ Himself – and that in judgement – combined with the belief that the Jewish nation rather than the Christian Church was the instrument which God would use for the establishing of his kingdom on earth, to discredit the concept of an established church. ... It became increasingly clear to Darby that the established church was apostate and ripe for the judgment, which was ready to fall upon it. Soon, he was to come to the conclusion that it was incumbent upon true Christian believers to withdraw from apostasy" (Rowdon, 1967, p. 53). Thus, his theology of the church in ruin was developed. Darby also believed that an understanding of the future events as he interpreted them must have a profound effect upon the lives of Christians. Apart from coming out from the established church and forming a unity around Christ, he considered that knowing

Christ was coming in judgement should cause Christians to "quicken their faith, to make them zealous and constant for him in their labours here; to separate them from the attachment to this present evil world; to lead them to be practically holy" (Rowdon, 1967, p. 52).

The movement which began with Groves was given impetus and theological interpretation through Darby. He laid the theological foundation upon which much of the proceeding work was based. Principles such as unity in Christ and the importance of the Lord's Supper find their source with him. Darby was also the father of the apostate church theology and the separatist exclusive movement, which also coloured the Brethren movement to its detriment. The Brethren movement spread quickly and began to blossom in two other particular places, Plymouth and Bristol, to which we now turn to see how the early thought was taken, developed and practiced.

PLYMOUTH

Benjamin Newton (1807-1899) and George Vicesimus Wigram came in contact with Darby in Oxford over a number of years. During that time Darby's effect on these men was profound. Both were convicted (in around 1830) to leave the established church and throw in their allegiance with Darby. Newton proceeded to invite Darby to preach in the churches of his hometown, Plymouth.

At that time, in Plymouth, a man named Percy Francis Hall, a commander of the coastguard stationed at Plymouth, was preaching doctrines similar in nature to those of Darby. Like Darby he acknowledged the authority of Scripture alone. Hall's major focus was on that of grace and love. He believed that a

21

Christian could not in good conscience be involved in war or the dispensing of justice, for all were called to be witnesses to the grace of God through the demonstration of the love of Christ. Upon his convictions, Hall together with Wigram, began a new work in Plymouth.

"Seeing the possibility of the establishment of a permanent work, Wigram acquired a chapel where regular preaching was to be given. The addresses were widely attended by Christians, both clerical and lay" (Coad, 1968, p. 61). The initial intention was to only establish a preaching centre for Christians, but it wasn't long before the Lord's Supper was taken in the chapel. "The Lord's Supper was observed; first privately by some half dozen who met for the purpose in the vestry on a Sunday evening, and then more publicly ... in the chapel itself" (Rowdon, 1967, p. 76). Darby writes of the same events: "More than once, even with ministers of the National Church, we have broken bread on Monday evenings after meetings for Christian edification, where each was free to read, to speak, or to give out a hymn. Some months afterwards we began to do so on Sunday mornings, making use of the same liberty, only adding the Lord's Supper, which we had, and still have, the practice of taking every Sunday" (Rowdon, 1967, p. 76).

The gatherings in Plymouth soon developed beyond the meeting of a few well-educated ex-ministers of dissenting and established churches. Hall's preaching was attracting many to the movement in the area. The group now contained many from all walks of life. Given the open format of the meetings and the many illiterate people now attending "it was felt that ungifted or otherwise unsuitable persons might be tempted to hold the platform. A presiding elder was therefore appointed to maintain order at the meetings and restrain any plainly unprofitable participants. B. W. Newton was the first to hold this duty" (Coad, 1968, p. 63).

Darby did not stay long at Plymouth but certainly played an apostolic role in its commencement and development. He said that he had seen in Plymouth more of what he was seeking than he had in Dublin – people acting together in unity. Through the addition of many talented men to the movement and the consistent enthusiastic preaching, evangelistic efforts, and communal atmosphere of the church, the "Brethren in Plymouth soon became a flourishing community. Already in 1835, they numbered about 80. By 1840 their chapel in Raleigh Street was too small and a large chapel, said to be capable of accommodating 1,400, was built in Ebrington Street" (Rowdon, 1967, p. 161). It is generally accepted that by 1845 there was a stable number of over 700 at Plymouth.

BRISTOL

With Groves leaving for Baghdad, Henry Craik (1805 – 1866) was out of a job. Moving to England he pursued studies in Greek and Hebrew and began to expound the Scriptures regularly. Craik moved to Teignmouth as a tutor in 1828. To Teignmouth also came a German named George Müller who had been trained for Lutheran ministry but became devoted to pursuing missionary work. Müller had come in contact with Groves in London and found much of what Groves taught in the ministry of Craik. Here "Müller experienced a change which he described as being 'like a second conversion'. He accepted the supreme authority of the Bible; ... and the necessity for a higher standard of devotedness" (Rowdon, 1967, p. 116). Müller married Groves' sister, Mary, and instead of moving to the mission field took up the position of minister at the Ebenezer Chapel at Teignmouth in

1830. While Müller was working as a Baptist pastor his thinking began to move toward those things which became associated with the Brethren. He believed that "it was Scriptural to follow the example of the apostles in Acts 20:7 and break bread every Sunday, even though no specific command to that effect had been given. At the same time, he concluded from passages such as Ephesians 4 and Romans 12 that opportunity should be afforded for any of the brethren to exercise in common worship of the church such spiritual gifts as they possessed" (Rowdon, 1967, p. 117).

In 1831, Craik left the work of tutoring and took up a position as pastor of a Baptist chapel in Shaldon, just outside Teignmouth. The friendship between Müller and Craik grew strong, both sharing a similar background, education, and now doctrinal approach to their work. The two often shared in joint preaching engagements. In 1832 Craik was invited to take up a position at an independent chapel in Bristol. But so close was the relationship that he had with Müller that he decided not to go to Bristol unless Müller also agreed to accompany him. Soon both decided to leave to minister together in the Gideon Chapel in Bristol.

Another opportunity presented itself for Müller and Craik. The Bethesda Chapel in Bristol became vacant and they were approached to use it to commence a congregation there. This they both saw as an opportunity to start a "new work from the beginning on the lines which had become a matter of conviction to them" (Coad, 1968, p. 44). The work continued to grow in both chapels throughout the year of 1832, and was recorded by outsiders to have been essentially the same as the work in Plymouth. During this year Darby visited Bristol and "preached in both chapels occupied by Müller and Craik and wrote appreciatively of the work that was being done there.... Thus already, contact had been made between the Dublin-Plymouth movement and that in Teignmouth-Bristol" (Rowdon, 1967, p. 121).

The first issue to challenge the work at Bristol was that of baptism. Should it be made a condition of fellowship in the church? Müller arrived at a conclusion, against other Brethren leaders elsewhere, that would serve "as the pivot of his views on the whole question of reception to the church fellowship. Müller decided 'that we ought to receive all whom Christ has received (Romans 15:7), irrespective of the measure of grace or knowledge which they have attained unto'" (Rowdon, 1967, p. 123). This decision, similar to the thinking of Groves in the early days, was to prove to be crucial to the direction of the Brethren later on.

The work grew to around 400 by 1837 and included by that time Müller's ministry to children and orphanages. Müller having similar convictions to Groves regarding the use of money and the need to serve the poor, began to develop an orphanage ministry in Bristol. The ministry began in 1835 in a simple way but grew rapidly incorporating a Sunday school work with it. From 1835 to the time of his death in 1897, "over ten thousand orphans had passed through his hands in sixty-two years. ... In addition, one hundred and fourteen thousand children had attended day schools and Sunday schools" (Coad, 1968, p. 53) under his supervision.

In 1839 Müller and Craik took time out to consider areas of church policy and discipline. They concluded that elders are appointed by the Holy Spirit, being confirmed to the church by them possessing the qualifications of elders and by their work being blessed. They took a strong line on discipline, seeing it as a community responsibility and that no delay in dispensing discipline was important for the health of the church. Regarding the Lord's Supper they concluded that it should be held each Sunday (Acts 20:7). "As to the character of the meeting at which the Lord's Supper is celebrated, since it is symbolic of common participation in the benefits of our Lord's death and our union to him and to each other (1 Corinthians 10:16,17), opportunity should be given for the exercise of gifts of teaching or exhortation and communion in prayer and praise (Romans 12:4-8, Ephesians 4:11-16). Though the meeting should not normally be in the hands of a single man, those who have gifts of teaching or exhortation should feel their responsibility to edify the church" (Rowdon, 1967, p. 126). These conclusions became the basis for the expansion of the work in Bristol and fell in line with and strengthened the growing work of the Brethren movement in England.

At this time Müller and Craik were still involved with the independent Gideon Chapel as well as their new work at Bethesda. However, many at the Gideon Chapel disagreed with the above conclusions reached by Müller and Craik. So, in 1840, not wanting to compromise their positions they resolved together to leave Gideon Chapel and concentrate their efforts at Bethesda in line with the beliefs and practices that they had determined. Müller summarised their position as follows: "We meet simply as believers in Christ, without reference to any sectarian distinction, maintaining the Scriptures as our only rule of doctrine and discipline and affording freedom for the exercise of any spiritual gifts which the Lord may be pleased to bestow"

(Rowdon, 1967, p.127). The work at Bristol had a large impact on that city growing to over 700 by 1840. The work also had a large influence on the work at Barnstaple commenced by Robert Chapman.

POWERSCOURT

Lady Powerscourt of Dublin, Ireland, had held several conferences in her home during the formative years of the Brethren movement. Many subjects were covered - prominent among them was that of prophecy. In September 1833, another conference was convened. Included among those in attendance were Darby, Bellett, Newton, Hall, Craik, and Müller. The very men who had figured prominently in the development of what became the Brethren movement met together to discuss many areas of theological interest. Common among them was a distress concerning the condition of the church of their day. They were grieved by the division of clergy and laity in the established church, the lifeless formality of the services, the lack of unity with the splintering of sectarian movements, and the lack of discipline and purity in the State Church. Darby, following these meetings decided that he could no longer be passive in these matters and was convinced that he should leave the established church and preach on his own merit. He felt that the church should never have the right to determine who could and couldn't preach or serve – that all spiritual offices come from God, not from the church. The 1833 meetings were by many regarded as "the commencement of Brethrenism" (Rowdon, 1967, p. 96). Following these meetings Darby preached all over Ireland, England, and Europe, expanding the movement.

THE EXCLUSIVE BREAK

What has been discussed above covers the important aspects of the emergence of the Brethren movement. However, there is another event, which is also decidedly important in considering who the Brethren are today. Newton, the leader at Plymouth, fell under accusation by Darby in 1847 of preaching erroneous doctrine regarding the person of Christ. Newton upon recognising his error published a statement renouncing his error. "This should have brought the matter to an end, but Darby dismissed the 'Statement' as a trick by which Newton sought to be credible and that he had not renounced his error, despite his clear profession to have done so" (Chase, 1989, p. 16). Darby's condemnation of Newton and subsequent rejection of Newton's confession proved devastating. "The result of Darby's campaign in Plymouth had been to destroy one of the most flourishing churches of the movement, and to drive into the wilderness one of its most brilliant teachers" (Coad, 1968, p. 151). This however was only the beginning of what eventually became a large division in the Brethren movement. The members at Plymouth refused to accept the denunciation of Newton by Darby, believing Newton's confession to be genuine. In response to this Darby forbade any Brethren congregation to accept into fellowship at the Lord's table any of the brethren from Plymouth, believing that other Assemblies could be led astray through the influence of Newton's erroneous teaching.

Following these events Darby, in 1848, was visiting the church led by Müller and Craik in Bristol. There he found some from the Plymouth congregation who had been admitted into fellowship at Bristol. At this Darby "protested and accused the Bristol Assembly of accepting those who were infected with the error of Newton and refused to have fellowship with them" (Chase, 1989,

p. 16). Darby this time had gone too far. "Müller and Craik were men deeply and widely respected for their outstanding Christian work" (Coad, 1968, p. 159). So, two parties developed, those who followed Darby enforcing the exclusion of any who came in contact with the Plymouth and Bristol Assemblies, and those who accepted all, following in the steps of Müller and Craik, and before them the steps of Groves.

Those who followed Darby became known as the exclusives – "their policy of segregating themselves from all with whom they cannot agree on what they regard as vital issues has resulted in a complicated process of divisions and sub-divisions. Those who ignored Darby's pronouncements continued to pursue what they conceived to be the original course of the movement. Continuing to practice the somewhat distinctive form of church life, which they believe to be required by the New Testament, they have nevertheless cultivated friendly relationships with all who are clearly Christian believers, welcoming them to every aspect of their church life on equal terms with themselves. ... They have been known as 'Open Brethren', often preferring to be called 'Christian Brethren'" (Rowdon, 1967, p, 264).

While the split between the Exclusive and Open Brethren was immediate and complete, that is not to say that the Open Brethren have not been at times and in various ways influenced by the thinking of Darby and others of the Exclusive movement since 1848. Much of what Darby taught within the united movement prior to the division had within it exclusive tendencies, which has affected in varying degrees the theology and practice of the Open Brethren.

Thus, the Brethren movement had begun and blossomed, to the point where it became clearly defined. Its development, growth and stand against the Exclusive division gave it its own identity, unique practice, and identifiable foundation principles. Next, we consider those practices and principles and seek to find those things that the movement has provided which should be retained, and how they should perhaps be contextualised today.

THEOLOGY

THEOLOGY OF THE BRETHREN

The distinctive theological emphases of the Assemblies grew out of the background, context, and historical events outlined above. The Brethren movement's focus on unity germinated in the environment of sectarianism, and it sought demonstration around the Lord's Supper rather than through conformity to structure or creed. The established churches' increased authority within the community saw them turn to the Bible as their only authority. They emphasised the importance of evangelism, sacrificial living, and evangelistic preaching, in the face of a self-satisfying established church. Discipline and purity emerged as important due to the apparent apostasy in the church. The power of the Holy Spirit was sought though spontaneity, for they could not find his work within the form and rigidity of the current establishment. The encouragement of each to express their gifts and a determination of no clergy/laity division was the reaction against the traditional structure and ministry practices, which were seen to restrict body life and the work of the Holy Spirit.

Having considered the story of the birth of the Brethren and its context, several theological themes rise to the surface, being shared by the fathers of the movement – these are:

1.   The unity of all believers in Christ.

2.   The authority of Scripture alone.

3.   The expression of gifts by all.

4.   The Holy Spirit edifies from among them.

5.   The call to sacrificial living.

While a complete theological discussion and conclusion on each of the above is not possible here, each shall be considered briefly in turn. We will consider the reason each aspect was important to the movement in the light of the context of its conception, and then briefly considers its validity now in view of current theological thought and the context of the church today.

UNITY IN CHRIST

It is no surprise that this theological principle was the first and probably the most important principle of the early Brethren. With the existing church splintering in all directions due to the apostasy of the established church, the Brethren led by Groves sought to find a place where the unity of Christ could be expressed in a non-sectarian way. Darby described the situation this way: "The division of the body of Christ was everywhere apparent rather than its unity. ... Borlase continued, the Church is not in a position in which she can exercise in any corporate shape the functions of the body of Christ" (Rowdon, 1967, p. 267-268). For the Brethren unity was not conformity, for conformity to the existing state of the church would only perpetuate its sinful state. For light to be effective it must be seen and for Darby unity within the church must be visible. He felt that "as long as Christians were satisfied with the cultivation of spiritual unity alone, the visible appearance of the Church must remain divided" (Rowdon, 1967, p. 269). Further, for Darby unity was more than a union of churches, which would again only serve to perpetuate the current sad situation. The pursuit of unity was for Darby a matter of obedience, to not pursue it was to disobey God's command. The Brethren also saw that a unity based around a creedal system promoted an intellectual unity which may not penetrate the heart and saw the current state of the established church as emanating from this very problem. A creed was also viewed as providing a barrier to free communion with all Christians and as being the instrument responsible for the schismatic state of the dissenting churches.

The Brethren felt that the basis for unity was to be found in and with Christ. For the individual, it was a life of sacrifice united with Christ in his death – dead to the world and to self. For the church, Darby found the solution in Matthew 18, "Where two or three gather together in my name, there am I in the midst of them." He placed this verse within the context of communion, which was taken as the outward symbol of union with Christ, and the unity of the Church. "Thus in his 'manifesto' of 1828, Darby wrote not only of the gatherings of 'two or three' but also of the partaking of the Lord's Supper as the outward symbol and instrument of unity since it is the commemoration of the death of Christ which is the means of gathering together in one, the children of God who are scattered abroad" (Rowdon, 1967, p. 288). For this reason, it was important to the early Brethren that the Lord's Supper be open to all Christian believers irrespective of their particular points of view on doctrine. As Darby says, "You are nothing, nobody, but Christians, and the moment you cease to be an available mount for communion for any consistent Christian, you will go to pieces or help the evil" (Darby, n.d., p. 18). For the early Brethren this principle of unity was expressed in the term "we accept all who Christ accepts" and was to embrace the whole church which Newton believed Acts 20:28 described as all for whom Christ had died.

For the Brethren unity was paramount and the acceptance of all became one of the most attractive attributes of the movement early on. It was to be found in Christ and expressed in the Lord's Supper. But questions remained. Who does Christ accept? What constitutes a consistent Christian, and is purity essential to unity?

One must bear in mind that these questions were considered within the context of what the Brethren saw as an apostate state of the church. Therefore, for Darby, discipline and purity became increasingly an important focus of his leading. Darby sought to withdraw from any sign of sin or evil or worldly system. Therefore, his answers to the above question were along the lines of, Christ accepts those who obey and strive to be pure - removing themselves from the effects of the world. Seeing the dangerous direction of Darby's efforts to separate from all whom he determined to be evil, Groves replied, "I would infinitely rather bear with all their evils, than separate from their good" (Coad, 1968, p. 25). The Open Brethren's position is reflected in Müller's statement:

"It is often said, for the sake of peace and union, we should not be very particular as to certain parts of truth; keep them back and treat them as matters of no moment. I humbly state that I entirely differ from this view; for I do not see that such union is of a real, lasting, or Scriptural character. ... Yet, while we hold fast the truth, all the truth which we consider we have been instructed in from the Holy Scriptures, we must ever remember, that it is not the degree of knowledge to which believers have attained which should unite them, but the common spiritual life they have in Jesus; that they are purchased by the blood of Jesus; members of the same family; going to the Father's house – soon to be all there: and by reason of the common life they have, brethren should dwell together in unity. It is the will of the Father, and of that blessed One who laid down his life for us, that we should love one another" (Coad, 1968, p. 275).

Today the basis for unity within many Brethren churches is a combination of Darby and Müller's position. Although initially the Open Brethren position on unity followed the work of Muller and Groves more closely - in accepting all who Christ accepts, the practice of unity has always found its basis in the spirituality of the believer – where Darby placed it. "As Darby developed his theology of the church in ruin, as well as his concept of separation from evil, God's principle of unity – the Lord's Supper - became not a symbol of unity but more of purity" (Smith, 1986, p. 87). The unity in Christ practiced initially by Craik and Müller, has through the influence of Darby become today largely a unity based on conformity to doctrine and practice, and even to a specific code of Christian living. So, the answer today to what is a consistent Christian, has been answered in terms of an individual's beliefs and purity. For the Brethren it became more important to hold right doctrine than to have spiritual life. While such an emphasis on purity has its rightful place, as soon as it overshadows a unity in Christ by the Spirit, then our focus is taken off Christ and placed on our own deeds, where we will always find division and disappointment.

The Brethren originally found their emphasis on unity not only in reacting to the sectarian movement of the day, but also firmly based in Scripture (John 17:20-23, Ephesians 4:1-6). In these passages one finds that unity is patterned on the unity found within the trinity. As the Father is in his Son and the Son reveals the Father perfectly, so also the Son is in us – through Christ's death, resurrection, and the sending of the Holy Spirit who draws us into him to unite us with him and to reflect him to the world. It is Christ in us that brings unity, not our state of purity. Further in 1 Corinthians 12:12-13 we find that the Spirit incorporates the church as the body of Christ. It is the Spirit who brings all believers into the church. The church is not the making of humankind but the creation of Christ, who through his death is evidenced now by the presence of the Spirit. If the church exists only because of Christ and is now given life by the Spirit, unity of the church will always be found only outside us in the life of the one who gives us life, namely Christ. "We are one people, therefore, because we are the company of those who the Spirit has already brought to share in the love between the Father and the Son. We truly are the community of love, a people bound together by the love present among us through the power of God's Spirit. As this people, we are called to reflect in the present the eternal dynamic of the triune God, that community which we will enjoy in the great eschatological fellowship on the renewed earth" (Grenz, 1994, p. 630). The issue is never how to achieve unity in the church, for it has been won in Christ. The issue now for the church is the demonstration of that which the church has in Christ to the world.

The Brethren certainly began with a freeing emphasis on unity, accepting all whom Christ accepts - those who confess Christ as Lord. However, in then seeking to find expression of this unity within the believer, the movement strayed in seeking holiness in the unholy, people. The basis for unity can only be found in Christ and in his work in us through the Holy Spirit. If unity is sought in what Christ has done for and is doing in the church, it shall be found. If, however, unity is sought outside that, in us, it will always prove to be elusive. The search for unity by conformity must end in finding unity in the only One who can be one and who has made us one in him. "Christian unity is a given fact of the new life to be believed and accepted by faith in Christ. It is not first the unity created, safeguarded, or enforced by a human institution or association. ... Like the righteousness of the Christian, it is found first and primarily and exclusively in Christ" (Elwell, 1984, p. 1128).

Can the Brethren today leave their desire for conformity, to reflect a unity of the oneness of the triune God, which incorporates diversity? "Christian unity is not identical to uniformity. It does not allow division. But it does not exclude variety. The one Spirit gives different gifts (1 Corinthians 12:4-5). In the one body of Christ there are many members. The unity grounded in Christ leaves scope for diversity of action and function, the only conformity being to the mind of Christ and direction of the Spirit" (Elwell, 1984, p. 1128). Can they return to a focus on unity in Christ by the Spirit, a free acceptance of all believers, rather than first searching for a standard of outward spirituality? Can they allow unity to be expressed through a creative and diverse body life rather than through conformity?

AUTHORITY OF SCRIPTURE

Together with unity, the authority of Scripture alone became a foundational principle of the Brethren movement. This foundational stance is not surprising considering the authority that the established church took for itself, often over and against Scripture. The thought that a system of tradition or church structure could in anyway determine the mind of God apart from Scripture was to the early Brethren, evil itself. And so, ,like many reformers before them, the Brethren sought to find the solution for church renewal within a biblical basis alone.

This principle is indeed commendable, important and correct. The church and indeed all things must bow to the authority of Scripture alone. However, this principle comes with presuppositional problems. All Scripture needs interpretation, and this presents among others, two main problems. Each interpretation contains personal presuppositions, and each interpretation is made within a specific immediate cultural and personal context.

Scripture for the Brethren was used to comment strongly on the current state of the church to the extent that its interpretation could now be construed on many points as an overreaction to specific contextual situations. For example, the stance on Brethren regarding structure and planning. Their belief that structure and planning produces evil and obstructs the Holy Spirit, was an interpretation arrived at only because those features were a part of a church that they believed was apostate. But today we can pose the question; was it structure and system that produced these problems or were they a result of other problems? For in many cases biblical warrants can be found for much of the practice of the established church although not condoning its condition.

One must also be aware that as soon as one interprets Scripture in a way which outlines a specific way of conducting church to the exclusion of the other, such as Darby did with his dead church theology, you yourself become open to being accused of creating a system from Scripture. This system must then stand condemned alongside the system you wish to react to or replace. Where the original Brethren "deliberately differed from earlier interpreters, it was often to impose upon Scripture their own system of interpretation, which rapidly hardened into as rigid a tradition as any other" (Coad, 1968, p. 250). The very thing that the Brethren movement sought to escape, the authority of tradition and church structure over the Bible, became the very thing that was created. This is inevitable unless all interpretation by the Brethren fathers was allowed to come constantly under scrutiny, allowing all tradition to be excised of any cultural and personal presuppositions embedded within the interpretation. The question must be asked, "Has this been the case?"

The answer in regard to Darby must be no. For he chose to impose his interpretations on the church to the end of purifying the church from all ill. Because he was a great teacher and a man of standing, he was able to influence many in many places. When confronted most notably regarding the Newton/Plymouth incident he pursued his line of thought to the exclusion of the unity of all – the result Exclusivism. However, Craik describes a spirit which "characterised the more tolerant among the leaders, when, in an address in 1863, he exhorted his hearers to first get rid of everything that superseded the authority of Scripture, and then with Scripture as the one standard of judgement, to make allowance for diversity of judgement" (Coad, 1968, p, 256).

This spirit which obviously existed among the first Open Brethren seems to have somewhat disappeared. The openness of which Craik exhorted has in many places, over time, been replaced by a calcification of tradition and uncontested interpretation. Therefore, one must wonder whether the Brethren believe in the authority of Scripture over the church or whether they mean the authority of an interpretation of Scripture over the church. Nathan Smith describes the situation this way: "All truth became nonnegotiable. There was no ambiguity in the Word of God, so although sincere and godly believers could differ, one must be wrong. This heritage permeated later generations with devastating results. The tendency was to separate rather than to compromise and division became a commonplace trait. ... The tendency then becomes to congregate around those of like values, both spiritually and economically" (Smith, 1986, p. 90). Thus, the bowing to the authority of Scripture has been replaced by bowing to an interpretation of it. This has undermined both the witness of Scripture among the Brethren through the destruction of the unity for which it began and served to narrow the diversity of the people within the church, thus limiting its effectiveness to reach people for Christ.

The result of such a focus has led to an arrogance in the belief that "we have the truth" and to a closed system of biblical interpretation, a system which does not allow beliefs and presuppositions to be confronted from within or from the outside. "I am inclined to think we have a spiritual problem more than any doctrinal problem. Our problem is spiritual pride. It is seen in an attitude that says we do not have anything to learn. It is seen in an attitude that is suspicious of anything that is new. It is seen in the attitude that insists that everyone must agree on every doctrine. It is seen in the attitude where we cannot tolerate differences" (Smith, 1986, p. 64). The problem is not with the movement's biblical authority stance, nor is it necessarily with Brethren interpretation of Scripture, but it lies in the insistence that their interpretation is right and in its exclusion of all else. Wherever this is the case any belief that one is bowing before the authority of Scripture must be questioned. How much more open and honest a position if the Brethren held that "if the principles believed are true, they will stand the most intense form of scrutiny. If the principles are not biblical or if our application of them is faulty, then we can only lose if we do not seriously listen to our critics" (Smith, 1986, p. 61).

Theologians name four bases of authority within the Christian realm: tradition, experience, reason, and Scripture. Theologians in the main seek to place any authority from tradition, experience, and reason as subservient to the authority of the Bible. The Brethren movement has sought to do this. Seeing a church which placed tradition above Scripture, it raised Scripture to its rightful position of authority. However, whenever the Brethren movement, or any movement, moves its own interpretation of Scripture to a place of being unable to be challenged, it creates its own tradition and places tradition above the Bible. At the same time the movement places its own interpretation above the work of the Holy Spirit.

All authority of Scripture comes to us through the work of the Holy Spirit who binds all together. Therefore, a confession of the authority of Scripture is by extension a confession of our "faith in the Holy Spirit who speaks his revelatory message to us through the pages of Scripture" (Grenz, 1994, p. 524). Historically the Brethren confession of the authority of Scripture has been based in the fallible instrument of the interpretation of humankind, rather than being placed in the infallible instrument, the Spirit. By placing the authority of Scripture in the work of the Spirit, the one who unifies the church, one also places the authority back into the body of Christ, the church. Thus, the interpretation of Scripture should never be an individual event but an ongoing activity of the wider body, committed to growing by the Spirit into the likeness of Christ.

If the authority of Scripture is placed in this community setting and is open to being challenged, it will never allow interpretation to gain the position of tradition and will ensure openness precluding personal pride and the dogmatism of individuals and traditions. Within the Brethren the Bible needs to find again a place to speak afresh, to confront our preconceptions and our context. There needs to be a place within our community where there is always an openness to being challenged with something new, a place that allows for diversity (such as Craik advocated), so that unity again can rise above a need for conformity, and the authority of Scripture can find its rightful place.

EXPRESSION OF GIFTS

The axiom underlying this principle is that God gifts all believers and all should therefore be free to exercise those gifts to benefit the church body. Few would disagree with this axiom. However, over time this principle became distorted. The initial movement in this direction was a movement toward freedom away from form and restriction. The original members of the Brethren movement were highly educated, many of them trained as church clergy in the Church of England system. They felt that the established church restricted the work of the Holy Spirit through the clergy system. By restricting those who could minister in the church to clergy only, the Brethren felt that the work of the Spirit in the church was being stifled. The early founders sought a freedom of expression of gifts within the church.

The initial and main focus for the expression of the gifts became the open worship time around the Lord's Supper. This provided a place for all believers (which became synonymous to all males after a while) to be priests before God and approach him around the Lord's table. Thus, the term "priesthood of all believers" became an important term for the Brethren. However, the expression of gifts by all in this forum, was actually the expression only of those with teaching and exhortation gifts, to lead the church in worship. So, while seeking the expression of all gifts, the movement only ever emphasised the expression of some.

This confusion regarding the use of gifts in the ministry of the church and the concept of priesthood of believers began to create problems. "Even though Scriptures clearly state that all believers are gifted, it is also clear that certain gifts which are more visible, and public are leadership gifts given to the church for the equipping of the saints (Ephesians 4:11-12). Problems developed when the concept of the believer priesthood was blurred with the public ministry gifts, so that it was determined that every male church member should have his turn on the platform preaching or ministering at the Lord's Supper. This distorted all the gifts. The verbal and high visibility gifts were valued above all the others" (Smith, 1986, p. 92). So, an over emphasis on freedom and the teaching and exhortation gifts led to a lack of distinction of the gifts and essentially an atmosphere where all were gifted alike.

This problem was further exacerbated by the tendency to confuse one's spirituality with the expression of the more public gifts. "The more one exercised public gifts at either the ministry meeting or the breaking of the bread meeting, the more spiritual they were thought to be" (Smith, 1986, p. 92). Thus, the freedom of exercising one's gift within the Brethren movement moved from, the right to exercise, to the compulsion to display your spirituality through participation in the public meetings of the church. Where this is true, one could say that in a very real way the so-called exercising of one's gift could be reduced to a display of one's spirituality. That is a movement away from the work of the Spirit, toward a work of our own. For the Spirit never exalts our spirituality but serves to exalt Christ.

This confusion of the priesthood of all believers, the exercising of gifts for the benefit of the church, and one's spirituality, must be confronted, and fortunately in many Brethren assemblies it has been. It is true that there is no biblical warrant for clergy to place a system of access to God between believer and their God. Nor is it true that only the clergy possess gifts and are therefore the only people appointed by God to minister in his church. All are priests and all are called to minister. In this line Berkhof (1970) states: "It is clear that taking the charismatic structure of the church seriously would put an end to clericalism and a church ruled by ministers" (p. 400). The Brethren in this regard have been well ahead of many other churches.

However, all do not minister in the same way (the direction the Brethren moved), but each are dependent on one another and the Spirit, to both form the body of Christ and to grow together in maturity. "So working together, each does his or her part toward filling the church with all the fullness of God, as Ephesians 3:19 puts it. In this regard, as seen from the whole, no one does more than a small part. And he or she can do that only because of the small parts of many others who each possess a charisma which they do not have themselves. Just as together we are dependent on Christ as the head, so together we are dependent on each other as members" (Berkhof, 1979, p. 400). A refocus on interdependence within the Brethren church would ensure that any focus on participation for spirituality points would diminish and place the gifts in their correct place of each doing their part to serve the body. In this way there would be a priesthood of all believers together with all the gifts functioning to grow the body worldwide.

If this were the case, then those with more visible leadership and teaching gifts would not be seen to threaten the freedom of those with less visible gifts. The over obsession with freedom of the Brethren, through the reaction to the rigid clergy structure, has led over time to a lack of appreciation and recognition of leadership gifts for fear of creating a clergy structure. But with all gifts given their rightful place of activity within the church this need not be a problem. For those with such a leadership gifting are then responsible for the "task of finding and involving the charismata in the work of the church as well as, where necessary, restraining those who possess them so that they indeed use the gifts for the common well-being. Without this activation and putting to work of the charismata, as well as discerning, testing and controlling them, the varied structure of the church would get lost either in uniform rigidity or in a multiform confusion" (Berkhof, 1979, p. 401). With a right emphasis on the gifts, leadership would ensure the right interplay of the gifts for the common good, thus leading the church, without creating a clergy system and without reducing the gifts to a "similar role for all", which can result in a church spirituality contest.

THE HOLY SPIRIT AND EDIFICATION

Together with the desire to allow all gifts to be exercised among them, the Brethren movement also felt that the Holy Spirit should be their teacher rather than the clergy of the established church. The thought was that any system is manmade and therefore replaces the work of the Holy Spirit. Therefore, the work of the Holy Spirit among them was seen to reside in the spontaneous exhortations by members from within the midst of those gathered. The Holy Spirit would edify his people as he saw fit to exercise the gifts among his people. The Brethren movement endeavoured to lay aside all form of structure or planning, for this was felt to be a hindrance to and foreign to the work of the Holy Spirit among them. "Any prearrangement and advanced preparation was considered a practical denial of the Holy Spirit's leading" (Smith, 1986, p. 92). The Brethren would then gather in the name of the Lord and wait upon the Holy Spirit to lead them and edify them spontaneously from among those gathered. Initially this was the pattern for any meeting that they held. Eventually this pattern was dropped from other meetings but remained the central theme of practice in the Lord's Supper meeting. This approach was seen to be the answer to the formal and lifeless services of the established church, where the life of the Holy Spirit could scarcely be found. In the context in which the Brethren movement began this approach provided immense freedom and gave much needed life to the church. But this view is not devoid of difficulties.

This view of the work of the Holy Spirit also precluded any seeking after training or biblical education, as it was again seen as a denial of the work of the Spirit and therefore only as the work of man. "The ironic fact is that almost all the early Brethren leaders had been trained ... some as top-rated scholars" (Smith, 1986, p. 92), and that it may just have been the theological training which gave rise to the founders being able to discern a new path for the church. This stance against training had little effect on the biblical teaching within the church during the lifetime of the founders. But although other cultural factors have compounded the problem, over generations the result of this anti-education stance has taken its toll on the biblical scholarship of the movement.

One must ask, has the Brethren movement created a theology of the work of the Holy Spirit within a particular context, which has produced a biased experiential theology? Did the founders experience a church dead through structure and planning, which led them to believe that the Holy Spirit cannot use structure and planning? Or was it the particular use of structure and planning, and the people involved, that produced the deadness rather than the functions of structure and planning themselves? The Brethren theology would lead one to conclude that the Holy Spirit cannot use any form of structure and planning. However, this very statement provides a structure within which the Holy Spirit must work, that is in the field of spontaneity. While the established Anglican Church limited the work of the Holy Spirit within structure and thereby reduced the freedom of ministry, the Brethren have precluded the Spirit's work in those same areas, thereby also confining his work.

The tendency with this theology is to attach a spiritual aspect to urges which come upon people when gathered together. To say that when one speaks that they have been led "without question" by an urge of the Holy Spirit is very dangerous. It places within a person who speaks the phrase "I was led by the Holy Spirit" an area of spiritual action which cannot be challenged regarding any self-based or sinful content. It also automatically attributes any activity done within this sphere of theology as automatically being attributed to and therefore indicative of the work of the Holy Spirit. However, all our actions are marred in some way by the sinfulness of our beings. Therefore, in a very real sense the urges and activities of humankind can shape our interpretation of the work of the Holy Spirit. For this reason, Barth (1993) states: "none of the external and internal 'urges' of our existence, as creatures that we know of, can be taken by us in themselves as they are as already the Creator's Word" (p. 9).

Therefore, we cannot say that all spontaneous activity is the work of the Spirit, for it may be the work of the flesh, or marred by it. Conversely, one may speculate that it was such hindrances by humankind within the structure of the established church that the Brethren actually reacted against. To be sure where the Spirit is there is freedom (2 Corinthians 3:17), freedom of relationship with God for all, but this freedom does not preclude any order. 1 Corinthians 14:26-40, which is taken by the Brethren as a blueprint for spontaneous edification, has as its intention the provision of a mandate for a fitting order. There is no biblical warrant for the exclusion of planning and structure, just as there is no biblical warrant for the insistence upon it. What is abundantly clear is that the Holy Spirit works through all people, in diverse ways, using the gifts that he has given them to build and edify the church (Ephesians 4:16).

An insistence upon spontaneity as the Holy Spirit's realm is no more than an insistence on another form, like clergy structure, which can just as easily be marred by sinful man and taken to be used for his own ends. One cannot prescribe the boundaries of the work of the Spirit beyond that of saying that he chooses to work through his people as he has gifted them. A correct emphasis on the gifts rather than any prescribed arena of operation will allow the work of the Holy Spirit to be further facilitated by the Brethren in the church.

SACRIFICIAL LIVING

From the outset the principle of sacrificial living, of living for others, was expressed and practiced among the Brethren. It is exemplified in the life of Groves, who spent his days on the mission field, and by the work of Müller among children and orphans. "Groves, Darby and others renounced wealth, comfort and worldly prospects in order to pursue a vocation of self-denial as missionaries abroad or at home" (Rowdon, 1967, p. 304). The established church had become to a large extent a class symbol. One aligned oneself with the church in order to move up in society. It largely represented the higher classes of society. The sectarian movement of the time also served to create a club atmosphere alienating the poor and oppressed. Against this church culture the Brethren movement refused state money and systems of raising money such as pew rents, preferring to trust God for all provisions.

While the Brethren church initially began with ex-clergy and associates, many who were rich, the movement soon became a movement for the people, including the poor and oppressed. Members saw that it was their duty to give up much to meet the needs of the poor in the name of Christ. "They renounced the possessions, pleasures and status of the world" (Dowley, 1977, p. 526). This became a defining mark of the early Brethren. As Groves stated: "It was the duty of everyone to give up all for Christ absolutely and unreservedly" (cited in Rowdon, 1967, p. 303).

The Brethren are to be congratulated for their efforts in reaching and serving the poor and for the example set in sacrificial living. Their desire to serve and reach others went largely unmatched. This was and still is "a natural extension of Jesus' own ministry as entrusted to us. Hence, in embarking on a ministry of service, the church is simply continuing the mission of Jesus himself" (Grenz, 1994, p. 660). However, as the focus on Darby's doctrine of separation from the world gained influence, the movement's sacrificial living for others began to become tainted by a separatist attitude to the world, which also meant a form of giving up anything that was seen as worldly. How subtle the shift was. Beginning as surrender to God's service, with and among the people, counting nothing for themselves, it changed to an exclusion from the world and its things, in order to count themselves as pure. The focus toward others began to turn inward toward self. In reply to this tendency within the movement which remains today in some quarters, Groves stated: "If ever there was a witness for God on earth, that witness was Jesus, and he never separated Himself from the synagogues; and this, if it proves nothing more, proves that separation is not the only way of witness, and yet he was emphatically 'separate from sinners,' not from their persons or their assemblies, but separate from their sins" (Coad, 1968, p. 264).

In some places the struggle for separation has undermined the movement's original philosophy of sacrificial living and giving.

Their movement to the world has been replaced in part by a movement from the world. The Brethren are not alone in the struggle to maintain a balance between separation and involvement in the world. This is the tension in which all of Christendom is placed. Without balance in this regard the church will end up following two lines – one to seek relevance through involvement in political and social arenas, the other to perpetuate previous forms and ideologies. As Moltmann (1974) puts it: "The more theology and the church attempt to become relevant to the problems of the present day, the more deeply they are drawn into the crisis of their own identity. The more they attempt to assert their identity in traditional dogmas, rights and moral notions, the more irrelevant and unbelievable they become" (p. 7). The first leads to the church being essentially no different to society and therefore having nothing to offer the world, the second leads to the church being irrelevant to society as it becomes too "other worldly". The church must be "in" to be involved and relevant, but not "of" to be different and therefore effective. It is this balance that the original Brethren had, but which in the main has been lost, and must be regained.

PRACTICE

THE PRACTICE OF THE BRETHREN

Flowing out of the distinctive theological bases of the Brethren are many equally distinctive practices which embody the movement's foundational theology. There is not room to consider them all here. However, it is necessary that the practice of worship in the Lord's Supper meeting be considered, for it is here that one meets the incorporation of much of the theology of the Brethren movement in the praxis.

This gathering of the Lord's people around the Lord's table each Sunday, which became the custom of the Brethren Assemblies, comprises three essential elements. Firstly, an open time where there is opportunity for those led by the Spirit, to exhort, teach, and lead the congregation in worship. Secondly, there is the partaking of the Lord's Supper. And finally, there is a time of teaching, where the word of God is expounded. From the earliest days these three elements formed the central core of the corporate expression of that which was important to the Brethren.

THE OPEN TIME

"We meet around the Lord at his table on the first day of the week, and at this meeting allow open ministry to any who appear to be led of the Spirit. The utmost simplicity of form is aimed at" (Bergin, 1913, p. 77). The open time of worship became the place where the priesthood of all believers through the expression of believer's gifts to edify all was expressed most clearly (for the Brethren the priesthood of believers and the expression of gifts became practically synonymous). The Brethren in seeking freedom from any structure and form felt that meeting without such hindrances meant that the Holy Spirit became present as they gathered and edified them from their midst through the gifts that he had given those so gathered. Therefore, this time became not only the place of gift expression, but also the place for the Holy Spirit to teach them through his spontaneous exercising of the gifts of those gathered. "The Brethren... believe that the Lord is, in a real sense, present in the midst of the congregation during this time of worship" (Webber, 1994, p. 11).

From the commencement of the movement the "original Brethren had excitedly involved themselves in new forms of worship – writing new music to fit new experiences and experimenting with new forms within the worship service. Some services at this time were prearranged, while others were more open, giving them a sense of flexibility and freedom" (Smith, 1986, p. 88). This flexibility, however, was soon removed and the format became fixed in the manner described above. The main reason for this was the theology of Darby, which forbade any organisation originating with man to be part of the services of the church. This pattern, which Darby insisted upon, became the tradition of worship for the Brethren. What was originally an expression of freedom, once insisted upon, became for many just

54

another form of bondage equal to that which the movement had reacted against. The Brethren were accused of exchanging a principle of freedom, which gave life, for a practice, which took it away. "Church life began to be stifled, until finally a non-written method of worship evolved which turned out to be more inhibiting and more predictable than prearranged services" (Smith, 1986, p. 88).

The importance placed on this service as the place where one expressed their gifts, served to suggest that all (meaning all men) should participate whether they were gifted in exhortation or teaching, or not. This, together with the emphasis on not preparing beforehand has led to a reduced standard of teaching among the Brethren over time, and a "constant and extremely wearisome recurrence of favourite ideas" (Neatby, 1901, p. 92). Edification among the Brethren, which began at an exceptional standard, due to the calibre and training of the founders, became diluted over the years in many places through the opposition to consistent training and forethought.

THE LORD'S SUPPER

During this open time the early Brethren believed that the focus of thought should be predominantly if not exclusively set upon the Lord's table and the significance of it. Therefore, this time was viewed as a gathering around the Lord's table. This gathering around "the Lord's table is for remembrance, for communion, and for testimony. As we sit there, we remember a face set as a flint to go to Jerusalem, mocked and spit upon, crowned with a wreath of thorns, bowed in agony of death, and exalted in resurrection glory. In our solemn remembrance, we have communion – blest comradeship with all the saints, and fellowship with God. ... And finally, to the world, we proclaim the

Lord's death until he come" (Bergin, 1913, p. 118). This Lord's table focus was the practical expression of the unity of believers, which was foundational to the Brethren. The gathering together without structure or prejudice of doctrine around the Lord's table in his name stood at the core of what the Brethren believed and practiced.

However, as previously mentioned, the focus soon moved from unity to purity, which had a large effect on the atmosphere in the Lord's Supper service. "The shift from life to light and the transition from the Lord's Supper as a symbol of unity to a symbol of purity caused the Brethren to assemble around the 'truth of remembering the Lord' rather than around the person and worth of the Lord Jesus" (Smith, 1986, p. 88). This shift from unity to purity in the meeting meant a shift of focus from outside oneself, in love, in evangelism and social concern, and toward community, to a focus of separation from anything that is not acceptable. Therefore, the Lord's Supper which initially stood as a symbol of unity, upon which the movement was built, was transformed into a symbol of a confession of purity in the partaking of it. The movement's original "acceptance and tolerance was an extremely attractive truth ... and a powerful testimony to the unity that they had as a practicing family" (Smith, 1986, p. 88). This, however, has been largely lost. That is not to say that the Brethren grew more and more unfriendly. Their friendliness remained, but a filter of acceptance guarded it. Acceptance became conditional upon one's purity. And one's acceptance in many places to the Lord's Supper was based along the same lines. So that which speaks of unity in Christ, the place where God calls all believers as his church to gather in unity before Him, has been turned into that which it is not, a place for division, separation and exclusion.

How can this remain in the church, whose ultimate calling is to community with God? As Gunton states, "Relations of human beings with the world are restored in a body [the church] whose prior ethical calling is the creation of a community of persons. Human fallenness is chiefly revealed in breaches of community... the sacraments of baptism and the Lord's Supper before all else operate to shape a particular pattern of community in the form of Christ" (1992, p. 113-114). Gunton in his exegesis of 1 Corinthians 11 states that the heart of the problem which Paul is addressing regarding the Lord's Supper is violation of community, not primarily a demand for complete personal holiness, for this is only found in Christ. He goes on to say, "offences against community are what invalidate the Eucharist" (Gunton, 1992, p. 113). This is why Paul says "It is not the Lord's Supper you eat" (1 Corinthians 14:20). It is not the people, or the content of the service, but the denial of community while celebrating the One who is community and who draws us into community to himself through his Son by the Spirit, which violates the meal.

The focus on community is why the Lord's Supper is linked with the eschatological supper of the lamb. "Meals are in almost universal human experience linked with notions of celebration and community. Food is best eaten in company, and so the Lord's Supper becomes the means by which the praise of God and the transformation of human life out of alienation and into the eschatological community are at once symbolised and realised" (Gunton, 1992, p. 115). If then the Lord's Supper speaks chiefly about community and the one through whom unity in community is possible, should not unity in community again be the focus for the Brethren movement? Rather than being a place where human imposed "purity acceptance" is carried out, which ultimately denies that which Christ has achieved for us on the cross, namely purity in him and in him alone, it must become a place where we meet in Christ, pure and holy as his body, unified and complete. Here the church becomes truly an eschatological sign to the world of that which is to come fully at his return. That is to be a place where purity and discipline is the response to the Christ encountered (Romans 12:1), rather than a prerequisite to the corporate encounter.

TEACHING

Following the communion time a time of teaching was common. This teaching time was often not planned. Someone from among them who felt led by the Spirit to teach would do so. The original spontaneous teaching practiced in the church initially functioned fairly well. However, when the strong leaders of the movement departed from the Assemblies this tradition posed a problem. Firstly, because of the spontaneous nature all were seen to be able to teach irrespective of gifting. "The concept of the believer priesthood was blurred with the public ministry gifts so that it was determined that every male church member should have his turn on the platform preaching..." (Smith, 1986, p. 92). Secondly, without any training or planned teaching program a well-balanced diet of teaching was unlikely to be achieved.

An acknowledgement of these problems over time meant that this practice has given way to a more structured teaching time. The speaker is often arranged before time, and in many places teaching programs are used. One must then ask, if it is seen that some structure is appropriate to assist the church in the formal teaching area, why is it not seen as appropriate in other areas? If structure is not bad, and can in some areas work more effectively than spontaneity, why is it shunned completely in other areas?

FUTURE

THE FUTURE OF THE BRETHREN

Because of the diversity of the assemblies of the Brethren today, much that has been considered above will not fit the position of all churches. This critique of the original Brethren and of the trends today has been written not to provide a complete and universal picture of the Brethren today, but more to provide a mirror of that which might exist now within the movement because of the paths chosen in the past. Suggestions of the possible areas which need consideration within the Brethren are made on this basis.

Having considered the context in which the Brethren movement came into being, and the genesis of it, and following the discussion above on the foundational theological principles and practices, one must now address the burning question: Where to from here for the Brethren? The answer lies in the recapturing of the original passions of the early Brethren, which in part has been discoloured and even lost over time. Considering this question in the categories in which the foundational principles and practices have been examined one can uncover a number of suggested directions for the Brethren in the future.

UNITY

"Unity by conformity to achieve a so-called purity and the need to be right distorted a beautiful principle of inclusive unity with diversity in the family of God" (Smith, 1986, p. 89). The Brethren should return to the foundation of unity "in Christ". To seek a place where diversity enhances unity and leads to a bigger picture of God in our midst. A finding of purity in Christ alone and a deep desire to reflect the community of the triune God in the body of Christ, the church, as the Holy Spirit works in each is required.

AUTHORITY OF SCRIPTURE

Among many there became an "unwritten and unspoken – yet powerful – need among the Brethren to be right. All truth became non-negotiable" (Smith, 1986, p. 89). The Brethren replaced the authority of Scripture with the authority of their interpretation of Scripture. A renewed embracing of the authority of Scripture and a desire to seek dialogue within community is needed to provide a way forward. The concept of a need to be right in order to be pure should be replaced by an open honest struggle with God's word within community as all bow together under the authority of the Holy Spirit to work in our lives. Here in this safe place of community we can allow the Scriptures to again confront and challenge our preconceived ideas afresh, providing us with a pathway to growth for the future.

EXPRESSION OF GIFTS

There needs here to be a right understanding of the priesthood of all believers, that all have access to God through Christ, and a freedom for the exercise of the gifts by all. That means that not all exercise the same gift, but that all gifts are given their place. Therefore, the public gift of leadership is not shunned for fear of creating structure but rather viewed as necessary to grow and direct the church. This will ensure that there is not a reduction of the body to a "similar role for all" approach to the gifts, but an emphasis on all doing their part for the common good.

THE HOLY SPIRIT AND EDIFICATION

Here the original Brethren have reacted against form and structure rather than to the way in which it was used. Thus, they formed a theology of spontaneity around the work of the Holy Spirit. This should be rectified. Any fear of form, or structure, or training, out of hand should be replaced with a healthy appraisal of how it is used. The Brethren need no longer confine the Holy Spirit to spontaneity but understand that the Holy Spirit works with and within all, whether in moments of form, structure, training, or spontaneity. Such a refocus will then allow the Holy Spirit to work through all the gifts, in diverse arenas of the church, to powerfully act as he determines.

SACRIFICIAL LIVING

The call to separation from the world is not a call to separate from the people, but unto Christ. The call to be among and to reach the people is as clear today as it always has been. The Brethren need to embrace that with which they began, a sacrificial movement to the world, without division, discrimination, or thought for self. A movement of mission and care for the world for the sake of Christ is needed. A movement toward the world to bring the world into unity with the One who unifies us to himself in Christ is also required. The future for the Brethren is the return to a movement toward the world with Christ, rather than a separation from the world altogether – for Christ never separated Himself from the world, but became that which the world represents, namely sin, for all. The Brethren movement must continue by being in the world to be involved and relevant, but not of the world to be different and effective.

THE GOAL

How can all this then translate into the practice of the Brethren Assemblies today? There needs to be a holding to the priesthood of believers together with a correct emphasis on the gifts of all believers as given by the Holy Spirit. By meeting in community in the presence of God as priests each is able to worship God through the expression of all gifts. This means that neither spontaneity nor form or structure is shunned, but both are used to express worship and to grow the church. The training of people in the areas of their giftings can be embraced. Likewise public leadership can be encouraged without fear that the work of God is being denied. But rather that it is being enhanced as each seeks to build up the body through a reverent submission to Scripture, which is constantly allowed to confront the beliefs and practices of the community of faith.

The Lord's Supper needs again to be the place of focus for true unity. It should again creatively take our attention to Christ, the one through whom God has reconciled all, rather than on ourselves and our own impurities. Thus, the movement is led to community, participating together as members of the body of Christ. As the meal is celebrated together there is a celebration of the Holy One who calls all to unity and community. And he who calls all into unity and community, into a relationship with himself, also calls all in their diversity to be conformed to Christ in their relationship with the world, to serve him by dying to self for the sake of the world and so to glorify his name in the world.

This must be the goal!

BIBLIOGRAPHY

Barth, K. (1993). *The Holy Spirit and the Christian life*. Louisville, KY: Westminster.

Bergin, Mr. (1913). *The principles of the "Open Brethren"*. Glasgow, UK: Pickering & Inglis.

Berkhof, H. (1979). *Christian Faith*. Grand Rapids, MI: Eerdmans.

Cairns, E.E. (1996). *Christianity through the centuries*. Grand Rapids, MI: Zondervan.

Chase, S.J.W. (1989). *The Open Brethren*. Th.M. thesis. Pasadena, CA: Fuller Theological Seminary.

Coad, F.R. (1968). *A history of the Brethren movement*. Exeter, UK: Paternoster.

Darby, J.N. (1971, reprint). *The collected writings of J. N. Darby*. Oak Park, IL: Bible Truth.

Darby, J.N. (n.d.). *Letters of J.N. Darby - 1*. London, UK: Stow Hill.

Dowley, T. Ed. (1977). *The history of Christianity*. Oxford, UK: Lion.

Elwell, W.A. Ed. (1984). *Evangelical dictionary of theology*. Grand Rapids, MI: Baker.

Grass, T. (2012). *Gathering to His Name*. Ayrshire, UK: BAHN.

Grenz, S.J. (1994). *Theology for the community of God*. Carlisle, UK: Paternoster.

Gunton, C.E. (1992). *Christ and creation*. Grand Rapids, MI: Eerdmans.

Miller, A. (n.d.). *The Brethren*. London, UK: Paternoster.

Moltmann, J. (1974). *The crucified God*. London, UK: SCM.

Neatby, W.B. (1901). *A history of the Plymouth Brethren*. London, UK: Hodder & Stoughton.

Rowdon, H.H. (1967). *The origins of the Brethren*. Vancouver, CAN: Regent College.

Smith, N.D. (1986). *Roots, renewal and the Brethren*. Pasadena, CA: Hope Publishing.

Webber, R.E. (1994). *The sacred actions of Christian worship*. Nashville, TN: Star Song.

www.ingramcontent.com/pod-product-compliance
Lightning Source LLC
Chambersburg PA
CBHW060355050426
42449CB00011B/2996